Cello Time Joggers

Piano accompaniment book

Kathy and David Blackwell

Teacher's note

These piano parts are written to accompany the tunes in *Cello Time Joggers*. They are an alternative to the cello duet accompaniments or CD, and are not designed to be used with those items.

Kathy and David Blackwell

MUSIC DEPARTMENT

OXFORD

UNIVERSITY PRESS

Contents

2.	Under arrest!	1
4.	Down up	2
6.	Fast lane	3
7.	In flight	4
8.	Lift off!	5
9.	Katie's waltz	6
11.	Rhythm fever	7
12.	Here it comes!	8
13.	Tap dancer	9
14.	So there!	10
15.	Rowing boat	11
17.	C string boogie	12
18.	Travellin' slow	13
19.	Tiptoe, boo!	14
20.	Lazy cowboy	16
22.	City lights	17
23.	Clare's song	18
25.	Chinese garden	20
26.	Summer sun	21
27.	On the prowl	22
29.	Ready, steady, go now!	23
30.	Happy go lucky	24
32.	Listen to the rhythm	26
33.	Cattle ranch blues	27
34.	In the groove	28
35.	Stamping dance	29
36.	Walking bass	30
38.	Runaway train	31
39.	Distant bells	32
40.	Lazy scale	33
41.	The old castle	34
42.	Rocking horse	35
43.	Patrick's reel	36
44.	Calypso time	37
45.	Cello Time	38

Cello Time Joggers

piano accompaniment book

Kathy and David Blackwell

2. Under arrest!

KB & DB

pizz.

Four short crot - chets
Four short quar - ter -

f stacc.

mp

played on G, (rest) one fell off and left just three. (rest)
- notes on G,

1   2   3,   (rest)   1   2   3,   (rest)   one   fell   off   and   left   just   three. (rest)

cresc.

mf

The cello book contains several cello duets; these are unaccompanied and so not included here.

Printed in Great Britain

OXFORD UNIVERSITY PRESS, MUSIC DEPARTMENT, GREAT CLARENDON STREET, OXFORD OX2 6DP

4. Down up

KB & DB

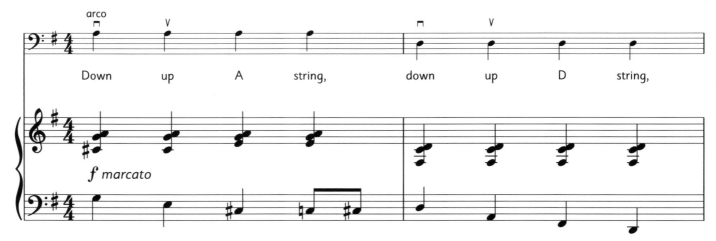

Down up A string, down up D string,

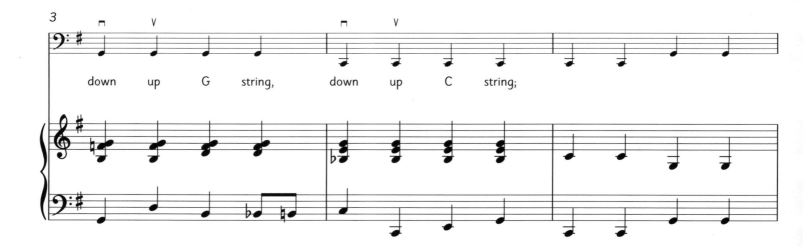

down up G string, down up C string;

Play the D and end with G.

6. Fast lane

KB & DB

Possibly faster the second time through!

7. In flight

KB & DB

8. Lift off!

KB & DB

9. Katie's waltz

KB & DB

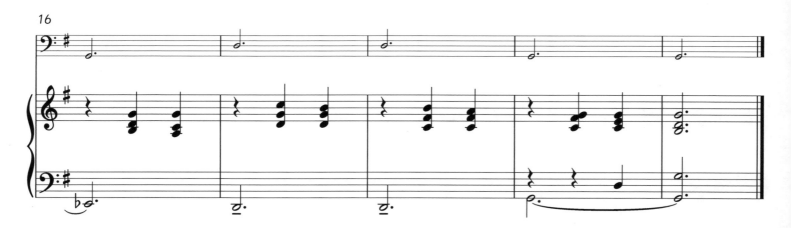

11. Rhythm fever

KB & DB

12. Here it comes!

KB & DB

Through the teeth and past the gums, so watch out, tum - my, here it comes!

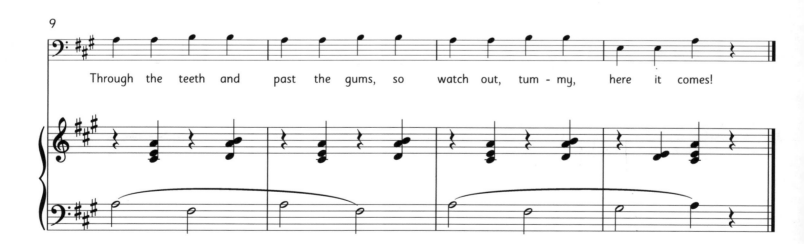

Through the teeth and past the gums, so watch out, tum - my, here it comes!

13. Tap dancer

KB & DB

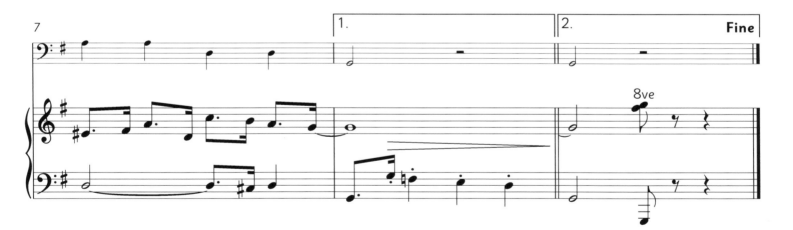

14. So there!

KB & DB

Brightly

So there!

15. Rowing boat

KB & DB

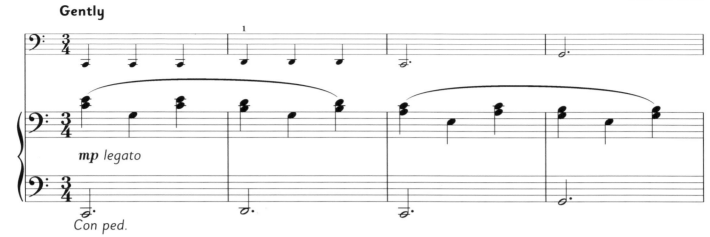

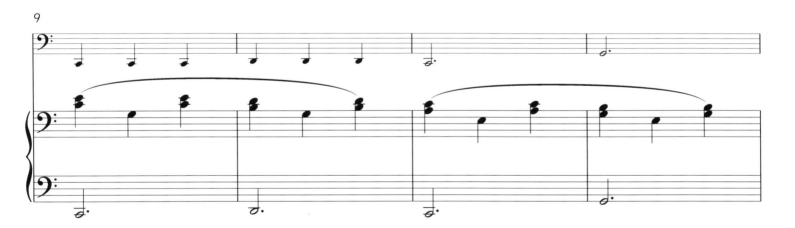
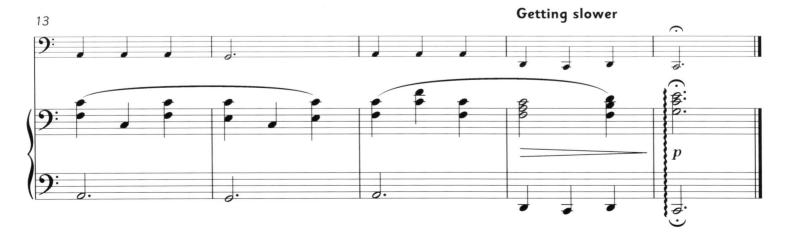

17. C string boogie

KB & DB

18. Travellin' slow

KB & DB

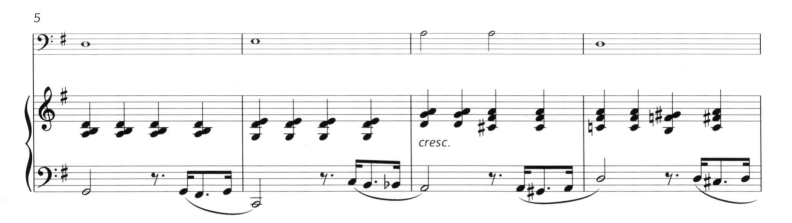

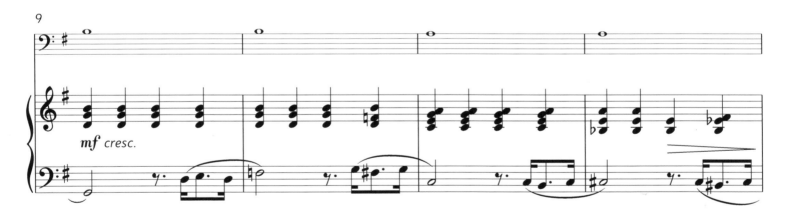

19. Tiptoe, boo!

KB & DB

Tip - toe   tip - toe   tip - toe, boo! (etc.)

In the cello book this piece is notated without key signature.

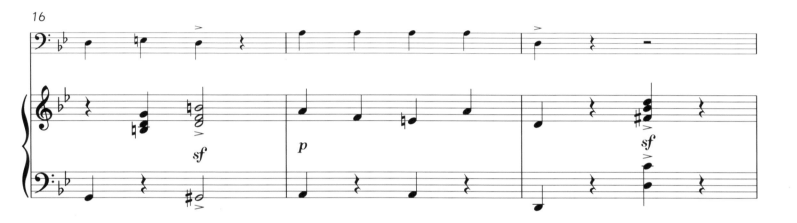

20. Lazy cowboy

KB & DB

At a gentle trot

mp

Con ped.

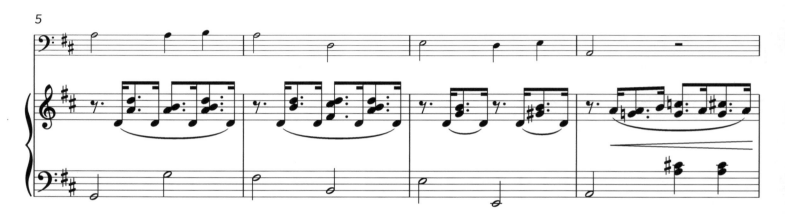

5

9

mp

13

mp

p

Ped.

22. City lights

KB & DB

23. Clare's song

KB & DB

Gently

5

9

14

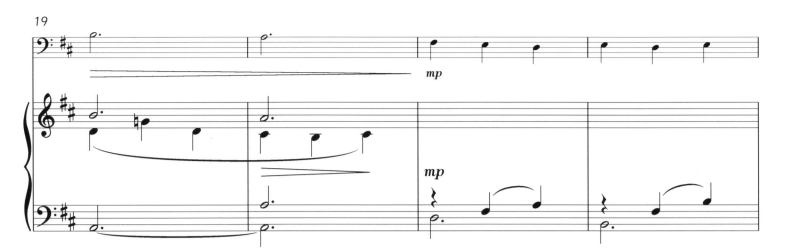

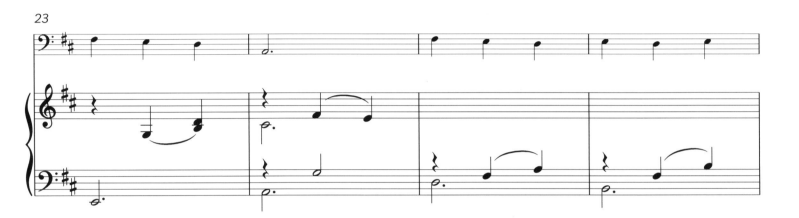

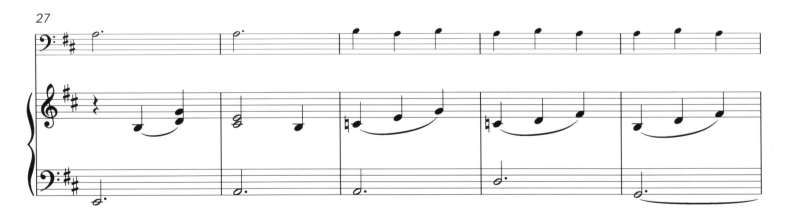

25. Chinese garden

KB & DB

Not too fast

26. Summer sun

KB & DB

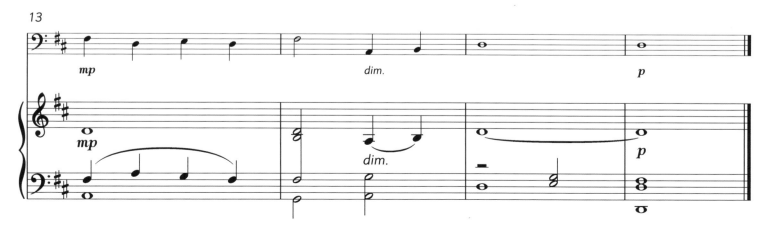

27. On the prowl

KB & DB

With menace

29. Ready, steady, go now!

KB & DB

30. Happy go lucky (for Iain)

KB & DB

Sunnily

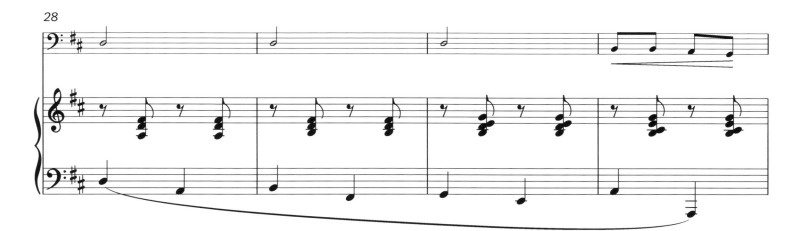

26

32. Listen to the rhythm

KB & DB

The repeat is written out in full in the cello part, which also includes alternative names for note-values.

33. Cattle ranch blues

KB & DB

34. In the groove

KB & DB

Swing

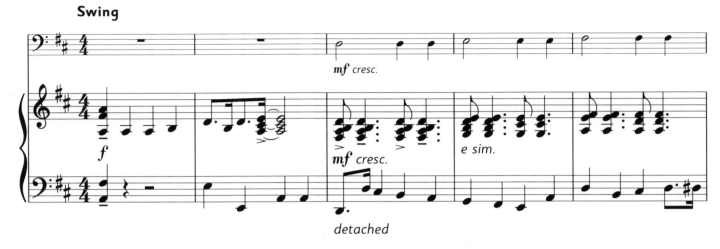

35. Stamping dance

Czech.

36. Walking bass

KB & DB

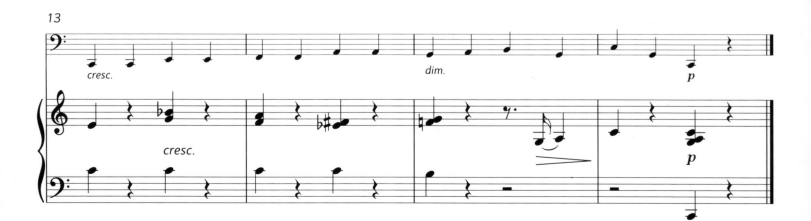

38. Runaway train

KB & DB

The music is written out in full in the cello part.

39. Distant bells

KB & DB

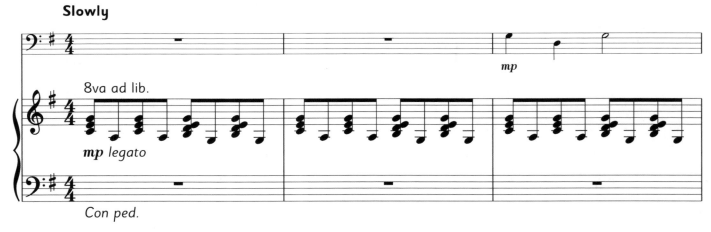

40. Lazy scale

KB & DB

Dreamily

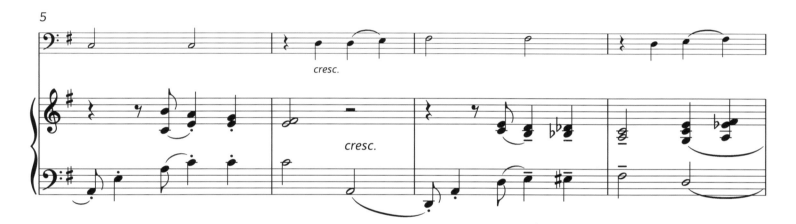

41. The old castle

KB & DB

With a singing tone

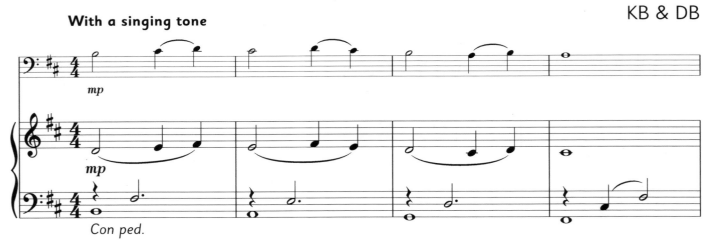

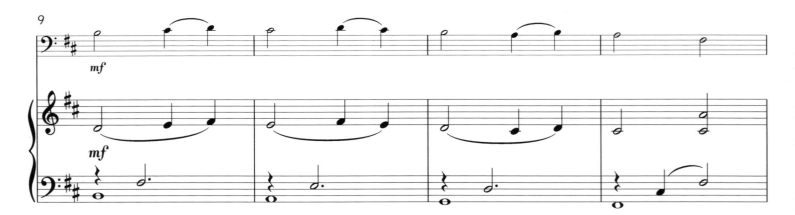

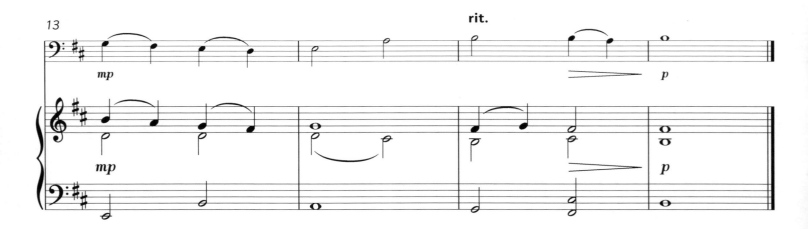

42. Rocking horse

KB & DB

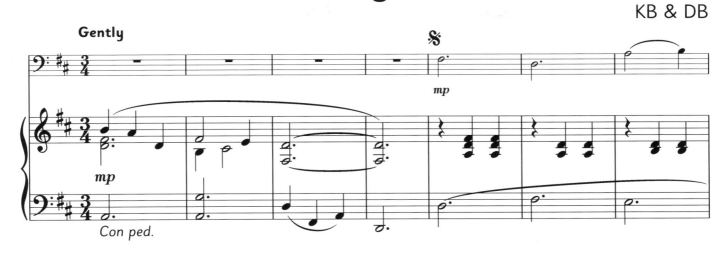

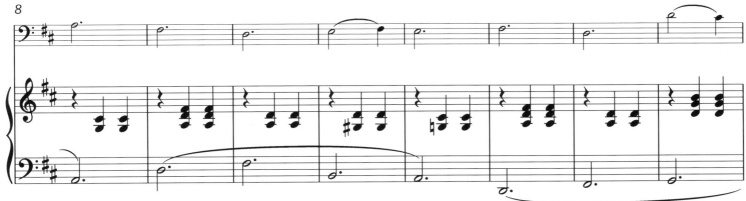

43. Patrick's reel

KB & DB

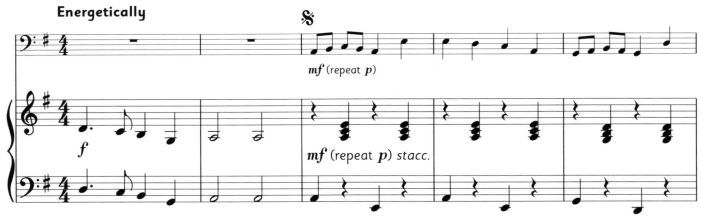

44. Calypso time

KB & DB

Carnival tempo

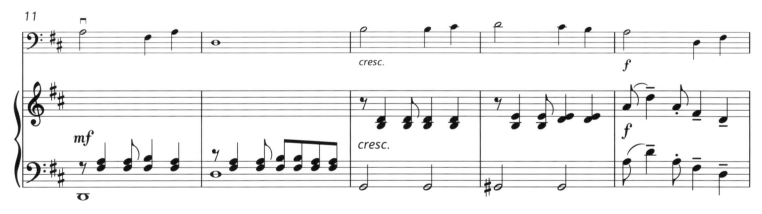

45. Cello Time

KB & DB

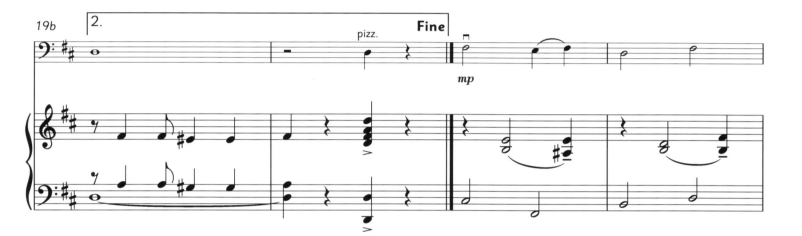